FOREST BOOKS

THE LAST ROCK EAGLE

BLAGA NIKOLOVA DIMITROVA was born in Byala Slatina, Bulgaria, on 2 January 1922. She completed her studies at the grammar school for classics in 1941 and in 1945 graduated from Sofia University with a degree in Philology. In 1951 she was awarded a Ph.D by Moscow University for her thesis 'Mayakovsky and Bulgarian Poetry'.

During the 1950s she worked for various periodicals and publishing houses as editor and co-editor, yet her main professional activity was writing. Among her numerous publications are: *Journey to Oneself* (Putuvane kum sebe si), a novel published in English translation by Cassell in 1969; the novel *Deviation* (Otklonenie) which was made into an international prize-winning film; and the once banned anti-communist novel *Face* (Litse). She has published more than twenty collections of poetry, and some of the poems have been used as texts for musical works such as *Spaces* (Prostransitva), *Impulse* (Impulsi) and *Voice* (Glas). She is also a translator from Polish, German, French and Ancient Greek.

Blaga Dimitrova is widely regarded as one of the most respected and popular writers in Eastern Europe and the CIS, and much of her work has already been translated into many languages. One of her translators, John Updike, described her poetry as 'breathless, oblique and resolutely personal'. She has already been awarded many distinctions as a writer, the latest coming from Austria and France. She had always felt under pressure during the communist hard-line regime and this increased dramatically in 1989 when she joined the 'Club for the Promotion of Glasnost and Perestroika'. At one point in 1991 she went on hunger strike for nine days in protest at the shortcomings of the new Charter. Blaga Dimitrova's past and present concerns for democracy led to her election as Vice-President of Bulgaria in January 1992.

BRENDA WALKER is a writer and translator mainly of Romanian literature. Her own poetry is published by Headland Press.

VLADIMIR LEVCHEV studied at the Bulgarian Academy of Fine and Applied Arts and is also a poet and translator.

BELIN TONCHEV, a graduate in English from the University of Sofia, is an author and translator.

ALEXANDER SHURBANOV was born in Sofia on 5 April 1941. He has a D. Litt. (honoris causa) from the University of Kent, Canterbury, and is a poet and translator of English poetry (Chaucer's *Canterbury Tales*, Milton's *Paradise Lost*, and Dylan Thomas), as well as author of books of literary criticism on Shakespeare and Marlowe. Alexander Shurbanov is Head of the Department of English at the University of Sofia, and is Chairman of the Bulgarian Society for British Studies.

FOREST
BOOKS
London & Boston

The
Last
Rock
Eagle

Selected Poems
of
**Blaga
Dimitrova**

*Introduced
by*
Alexander Shurbanov

*Translated by Brenda Walker with
Vladimir Levchev and Belin Tonchev*

FOREST BOOKS

20 Forest View, Chingford, London E4 7AY, U.K.
PO Box 312, Lincoln Center, MA 01773, U.S.A.

FIRST PUBLISHED 1992

Typeset in Great Britain by Cover to Cover, Cambridge
Printed in Great Britain by BPCC Wheatons Ltd, Exeter

British Library Cataloguing in Publication Data:
Dimitrova, Blaga
The last rock eagle.
1. Title
981. 8113
ISBN 185610009X

Library of Congress Catalogue Card Number:
92–72166

Forest Books gratefully acknowledge financial support for this
publication from the Arts Council of Great Britain and the Open
Society Fund, Sofia.

Contents

Introduction

'Your poems. Are they difficult?'

She smiled and, unaccustomed to speaking English, answered carefully, drawing a line in the air with two delicately pinched fingers holding an imaginary pen: 'They are difficult – to write.'

He laughed, startled and charmed. 'But not to read?'

She seemed puzzled by his laugh, but did not withdraw her smile, though its corners deepened in a defensive, feminine way. 'I think', she said, 'not so very.'

A glimpse of Blaga Dimitrova snatched by John Updike, an amused traveller across Eastern Europe way back in the sixties. A recognizable image, revealing in a single stroke so many of her unmistakeable characteristics both as a person and as a poet: the fine poise, the mixture of spontaneity and sophistication, of openness and quick withdrawal, of confidence and vulnerability, of trust in the outer world and a constant concern for the preservation of her inner territories. And, above all, the awareness of the protean nature of words and the urge to play with them in a lighthearted and yet terribly serious way.

Words are especially dear to Blaga Dimitrova, because in a world of interdictions it is only among them and in them that she can be truly herself. 'If they should put a ban on my words, how could I quench this thirst of mine?' This ultimate deprivation is what she has feared the most and the recurrent images of the severed, mutilated or imprisoned tongue in her poems lend physical dimensions to her lasting anxiety.

But, of course, words in themselves are nothing. What gives them worth is the spirit that flows into them and makes them live. And it is this spirit that Blaga Dimitrova is concerned about. In an age of collectivistic dogmas, she was among the first Bulgarian intellectuals to see through the general illusion of 'all are equal' and its shameless abuse by the few more equal than others, and resolutely depart from it in order to raise against it the subversive ideal of individual freedom.

Freedom has been a preoccupation of this poet since her early days. At first, a romantic yearning for a fuller life, a continuation of the dreams of an older and well-known Bulgarian woman poet, Elisaveta Bagryana, for a feminist emancipation, it gradually grows into a basic law of existence, whose violation is fraught with danger. Freedom, in that deeper sense, is no longer seen simplistically as a way to heavenly bliss. Its repercussions can be dramatic and even tragic, but without it humanity can never reach fulfillment.

The theme is first sounded in her amatory poems, which were published in the late fifties and at once established her as a major figure in the national literature. Here the woman in love pleads for a new relationship between the sexes, in which she would not seek shelter under somebody else's wing but would instead be helped to spread wings of her own. Such partnership, of course, is not readily available, and in the event the poet sees herself as a lonely traveller challenging the age-old fears and prejudices of the tribe yet remaining true to herself. This turns into a central image in Dimitrova's poetry. She learns to face on her own both the social wrongs and the mysteries of the universe which surround her. She learns to admire the rare gestures of personal integrity and defiance of outward pressures in her contemporaries and eulogize them as heroic. And she becomes intensely aware of the autonomy of the individual, hence of the finest movements of the soul, which find expression in such delicately insightful poems as 'Touch', 'Under the Snow', 'An Old Song . . .', 'Tomorrow', 'Repentance'. A fundamental paradox of the human predicament is discovered and has to be accepted: boundaries are the prerequisite of contact. And, consequently, the only ideal social model is contained in Bach's harmony, which manages to weld together 'free, independent, varied voices into a prayer-like, sovereign unity of spirit'.

It is this model of a better world that Blaga Dimitrova has been trying to approach with an admirable single-minded-ness through the years of hardships and trials. First of all, within her own self. The stumbling-blocks in her way have been many and she has indeed turned them all into a mainstay; the stormy clouds of adversity have paradoxically provided her with an impenetrable armour. And she has withstood the temptations of the world no worse than Spenser's Britomart of Milton's Chaste Lady. When many a manly voice reduced itself to the squeaky pipe of sycophancy, her womanly voice remained gentle yet intransigent. *And more, much more than that*, she drew the prohibited outer world into herself, compressing and sublimating it into poetic visions. Thus the great centripetal force of her talent internalizes everything that appears to have a detached and ominous existence, like the ringing of the midnight bell, the Great Chinese Wall and even Fate herself, who, it turns out, can only 'knock on the door with your own hand'. This is what makes one equal to the world and, therefore, free.

The worst they can now do to you is to try to stifle your voice. But the word shackled by the goaler of authority develops its own painful ways of continuing to exist through the manifold indirections of suggestion. Enforced immobility makes it rather taut and heavy, but then each little movement becomes a distinct signal that keeps the reader alert and attentive.

In the early eighties, Blaga Dimitrova was translating the work of a contemporary Swedish poet, and during a chat over coffee she told me that Scandinavian poetry struck her as amazingly clear and translucent – like a Northern lake on whose bottom you could see every tiny grain of sand. She was envious of that absolute intellectual serenity unblurred by the turbulence of passion. Some of it, I feel, she has now achieved in her own, more Southern way. Her poetry has more and more veered away from direct emotional effusion towards greater reflectivity and self-analysis. But this rational orientation has not robbed it of sensuous immediacy. In Julia Kristeva's words, 'Blaga Dimitrova can turn thought into poetry, meditation into rhythm and flavour, colours into ideas, judgment into fragrance, vision into ethical statement. Seldom has a woman's writing been at once more cerebral and more sensual. This mixture comes about no doubt like visions brought on by a wound, personal or national.' We could now add: *or both*.

Thoughtfulness in art is almost invariably a sign of dissatisfaction and dissent. So is the divestiture of poetry of its traditional harmonies of metre and rhyme and melody, its adjustment to the accents of the everyday, its assumed 'prosiness', its irreverent play with the word and the sentence. In her country, Blaga Dimitrova, a recognized mistress of classical verse, was among the first who dared take these suspicious new paths, and the poetry police was not amused. Its line was to play such developments down, to hush them up, to present them as marginal and insignificant. But the intelligent reader, of course, knew better than that.

For a poet to do in the medium of language what Blaga Dimitrova has done both as an artist and as a shaper of the public mind, in a period of strict totalitarian control of the arts, is more than enough. But to turn into a *national* poet, by the standards of the Bulgarian tradition, you must be ready to take yet another crucial step – from the world of prophetic dreams into that of actual events – and make your proudest poetic words good there. Blaga Dimitrova is one of the very few who have passed this difficult test as a leader of the anti-dictatorial dissident movement before 1989 and as a prominent figure of the popular opposition against the devious attempts of the former rulers to retain their power under a variety of new guises since then. Her fight has been singularly triumphant, and she is at present the Vice-President of democratic Bulgaria. In her striking progress she has repeated the life journey of one of the fathers of modern Bulgarian poetry, P.R. Slaveikov, who was also an eminent educator, folklorist, translator of the Bible, editor of journals and fighter for national independence, and who was elected Chairman of the country's first parliament after its liberation in 1878.

This is all very heartening and speaks for the people's continuing respect for their spiritual leaders. Yet, in a more normal situation, I feel, politics should be taken care of by politicians and poets should be left alone to write their poetry – as individuals, free and solitary, among the multitude of other such individuals who need their encouragement. I am sure that Blaga Dimitrova is working towards that goal. For a little longer. Just having to be there. Giving it all another push. Gently but firmly. In the right direction. Putting her resonant words to the ultimate test. A poet in power – a dangerous oxymoron.

Alexander Shurbanov
Sofia, 1992

We are indebted to Blaga Dimitrova for her close
collaboration and guidance in these translations,
selected mainly by Belin Tonchev.

The Poems

В УСТНАТА КЛЕТКА

Как позволи езикът ти —
див, необязден, прескачащ
през стобора на зъбите —

да бъде опитомен?

Той си ближе думите,
както раните — тигър
в клетка под ключ.

Призванието внезапно
се разлютява в кръвта му
и тъкмо да изригне рев —

Надзирател на себе си,
яростно се захапва сам.
Руква мълчание.

Зад зъбите езикът кърви.

(1988)

In the prison cell of the mouth

How did you allow that tongue of yours –
wild, unbroken, leaping
over the toothed fence –

to be tamed?

It licks words
like a tiger licks its wounds
but in a locked cell.

Vocation suddenly
boiling in its blood
a roar about to erupt –

Its own jailer,
fiercely biting into itself.
Silence streams down.

Behind the teeth the tongue bleeds.

(1988)

Eagles are vanishing

With the extinction of animals
something human also vanishes forever.

The last rock eagle
has circled for the last time.

He felt a taste of parting in his beak.
What unsolved secrets
did he tie into a faint knot?
What rooted him out of the sky?
Was it lack of air
to breathe and spread his wings?

At dawn who will create
those high outlines of freedom?
Who will continue those flowing circles?
Who will first foresee in the distance
the pirate sails of a hurricane?
Whose eye will be faster than the lightning?
Who will stir the reed's flute
with the beat of wings?

Who with one swing will open infinity
above the towers of crags,
into the eye of the well?

Who will show youth
how to fly against the wind or in no wind?
Who will pierce
the cold breast of the rocks with his claws
to feel the cohesion of the planet?

Who will send me a brave feather
from the clouds plucked out by a storm?

4

The last rock eagle
has circled for the last time.

The azure's smile has frozen
above the rocks and rocked hard.
The comparison 'like an eagle'
has lost all meaning.

(1983)

Introduction to the beyond

Expiring fully conscious,
you mustered enormous strength
to die peacefully,
without any cry, or moan, or shiver –
so I'd have no fear.

Carefully, your hand
grew cold in my hand
and imperceptibly led me
into that beyond to death
just to introduce me.

In the past, and as carefully,
you used to hold my small hand
and lead me through the world,
show me life –
so I wouldn't be afraid.

I'll follow you
with the trust of a child
to that silent country
where you went first,
so I wouldn't feel strange there.

And I won't be afraid.

(1966)

Bach's harmony

Bach gave equal rights to every kind of voice
and no voice was allowed to be inferior,
having to serve as an accompaniment or background,
in order that a privileged voice might excel.

And therefore, through the ages, shall go on sounding
that pure, supreme harmony, welding together
free, independent, varied voices
into a prayer-like, sovereign unity of spirit.

(1983)

Frost

To Todor Borov

The arrested day is peeping
through bars of frost.

No sparrow dares fly over
the barbed wire of the air.

And the sobbing throat of water
is stopped up with a lump of ice.

And our steps in the snow
are clanging with chains.

For us, there is only one possible escape
from the white prison of winter:

to be our own freedom.

Dispute about poetry

We were sitting on the shore of the day – two poets,
engulfed in a dispute about what is real poetry, and
myself who listened to them in silence.

'Poetry,' one of them insisted without a shadow of
doubt, 'that's simplicity. At long last we've got to pull it
out of the whirlpools of intricacy!'

'On the contrary!' retorted the other, equally convinced,
'Poetry is entangled in the mud-banks of elementalism.
We have to drag it to the depths of intricate thinking!'

The dispute was lashing first against one shore and then
against the other, getting foamier and foamier.

A dragon-fly began to circle between the two,
(its fine wings carried the faint smile of its last sun-eyed
day) then darted straight for the evening.

The dragon-fly was neither simplicity nor intricacy.

It was poetry.

(1984)

Midnight bell

An aural hallucination,
Sound-ghost . . .

Boris Pasternak

It's night again. And an even more
uncertain uncertainty.
Sleep runs away from the eyelids
    as if stung.

You wait, listening alertly.
smoothing the bedding
again and again,
    as you did your husband's grave.

And just when everyone's asleep,
you rend the clean sheeting
of silence with a hoarse shriek:
    – Who's ringing the bell?

And shivering you half open . . .
Framed in the doorway
standing full length on the threshold
    is darkness.

For a moment you stare at each other
just stare, point-blank. Dumbfounded.
As if you knew one another,
    But from where?

A rapidly slammed door.
A frightened whisper:– It's no one!
The noise of slippers coming back.
    Another stepping on them.

Then for a long time, all by yourself,
amazed, staring into the emptiness
you ask out loud:
          Who rang the bell?

(1979)

Heroics

To some intellectuals et al

I'd lose all confidence in the future,
if I didn't know people who'd lost their future.

They could, but they don't want to get rich –
grasping their innocent poverty parsimoniously.
They could, but they don't want to find fame –
they're proud enough having chosen to be a nobody.
They could – with hardly any effort –
but don't want to, climb upwards.
They've taken the road – what a feat!
downwards, downwards – to the peak of the root.
And on from there to discover the hidden prospect
of blossom and fruit – still at the pre-embryo stage.

Nameless naive ones who have lost their future –
without you I'd lost all confidence in the future.

(1972)

Grass

I'm not afraid
they'll stamp me flat.
Grass stamped flat
soon becomes a path.

(1974)

Self-portrait

So you want to be an icon
  with an iconoclastic image.

Eyes, short-sighted for things no further than your nose,
  staring at things in the distance
  which cannot be seen.
Lips with a nondescript shape,
  thirsty, cracked,
  without knowing why.
A smile, resembling a grimace of anguish,
  an anguish, resembling
  a smile.
Gestures like somebody drowning.
  You feel your neck closing in on you,
  and your fingers opening out.
A carelessly free gait, always against the wind,
  creating your own
  cross-wind.
Belongings – countless numbers of lost umbrellas
  and a couple of words
  found minus their armour.
An untidy house, suitcases ready for a journey.
  An uncertain itinerary,
  a certainty in change.
A mind, that doubts the obvious,
  having blind faith
  in the improbable.
Loneliness when at the age of love,
  love when at the age
  of loneliness.
A shoulder, standing on end, ready to butt
  the closed door
  of the air.

Hands, which let go of everything
    in order to catch hold
    of the wind's beard.

Now travelling lady, what's your mainstay?
    The stumbling-block, perhaps.

(1974)

A bird's lot

Pseudo free bird!
Since first memory
you've yielded blindly
to the tyranny of song
(just in case it was considered song).
It has seized you by the throat,
worried life out of you through your teeth.
It drives you out
against the wind's command,
under the guillotine of the rain.
It throws your nest and world
into disorder.
A millstone round your gullet –
your talisman.

You pseudo bird of God!
       Singing the way you do
      the song only makes you cry.
        It darkens
         your brightest day,
       turning your black
         feathers white.
        Your perkiness –
        to dust and ashes.
      Your aggressiveness –
        to soot and rime.
        Your enthusiasm
        to dirt and fumes.

Pseudo migrating bird!
Do you hope to escape further south
from your shivering with cold?
Here is your fiery south,
Don't fool yourself:
You don't patch up your song,

the song patches you up,
weaving noose after noose,
suddenly after suddenly,
mouth shut after mouth shut,
the cage of your life
(just in case it was considered life).
Are you tapping on the window
waiting for crumbs of love?

Pseudo song! Pseudo innocent!
A thorn in the eyes of the blind –
mafia of philistines.
A position on a sawn-off branch.
A flight into fall.
A challenge to the wind.
A sting on the heel of Achilles.
A singing sleeplessness,
while everything is sleeping.
A naked cry: 'The King is naked!'
Insane assault with the sabre of a beak.
A cherry-tree cannon,
twit! tweet! twit!
Feathery nitwit finery.

Pseudo Firebird!
Many live in fear
that you may set the forest alight
with a sun-dipped feather.
The song of the stone in the sling
will betray you.
(A yellow-beaked mob lie in wait.)
You can't atone with a stone!
Turn to the cloud –
it promises a storm:
What armour!

(1975)

17

Chinese wall

I recognised it at first sight, and it – me.
Step after step
straight upwards
along the thousand-year-old toothed wall.
I didn't need a guide
or a language for misunderstandings.
Gropingly, I was lead by the umbilical
protocord.

I was curious through embrasures of loop-holes.
Beyond,
as if the same, innocent grass
and mountain and forest and sky,
yet entirely different:
alien, forbidden, dangerous –
haunts of horrors.
The wall had marked
the ridge of fear.

For a long time, I walked the back of this stegosaurus,
rising from horizon to horizon,
from epoch to epoch,
shutting out the air,
crossing out the landscape,
stopping the echo.
Only time like a grass-snake
wriggles, unhindered through it
second by second,
spasm by spasm
century by century.

I patted the stones intimately
and spoke to it silently:
You were embedded in my cells
long before I was born.

Your embrasures
are my eyes to the world,
half-closed with suspicion.
Your walls are cemented
with my blood, sweat and tears
stone upon stone,
fear upon fear,
silence upon silence.

How many millenia of eternity will I need
to tear you down within me?

(1966)

Touch

Everything is divided up with boundary line,
which is a contact to something else.

the stem is imprisoned in bark –
Through it, feels both wind and rain.

The fish is armoured with scales –
through them it senses the sound of waves.

The sea is clamped by shores –
through them it touches the thirsty land.

I am nailed within a woman's skin –
through it I know caress and wound.

We contact the world
only through our boundaries.

And in becoming more boundless,
we will become more lonely.

(1988)

Brand

It's your own hands
that scar you
with an ember:
tongue-warrior and tongue-creator

Which means –
to cut off your own bare tongue
with the blade of the tongue

right back to the plaited roots.

And to start sounding out an *a–b*
because suddenly
it's essential as daily bread,

(unsupervised like laughter),

that the chain-like curse
of the withered tongue
is impaired.

(1986)

The River Yantra

It springs from my childhood.

In the river on a death bed –
still fluttering
the sky bleeds from sawn off wings.

Suddenly everywhere's brighter,
by one more teardrop.
A felled shadow recognised me.

I peep from the river bank into myself.
The water dryly refuses
to reflect my face.

(1988)

Pacification

So many humiliations –
in one day.

But not
everything
shows.

You see there's something
invisibly small
greater than anything else.

It's there with me
out of nowhere,
indestructible.

An anticipation that . . .

And however much it loses its way
it can never go further
than myself,

which is – beyond time.

(1988)

On the wane

When the moon is on the wane,
it's near to waxing.

I remember that old saying
from childhood

But what if earth were on the wane?
No one ever spoke of that.

They just never conceived
the possibility.

So I'm left to guess –
a full-earth or a void?

(1988)

Face to face

Sat facing each other
we talk around
the main topic:
if – otherwise – actually.

And I wheedle it out of myself:

Who speaks the truth?
The words or the silence.
The look or the voice.
The gesture or the hand.
The pose or the spasm.
The distance or the proximity.

We sit facing each other
with our backs to ourselves.
With hired faces,
a half-word from truth.

We get the meaning.

(1988)

Reflections in moonlight

The moon floats
from one look to another
with a bitten cheek bone.

And light drips.

To think yourself
pure as a lily
means you've never merged with others.

And even blinder,
in your own sterility,
you're stained, pitch black.

(1988)

End of the century

The coat of arms of my setting century
paralytic with frenzied speed,
sclerotic in memory banks,
turned blind by laser pupils,
turned deaf by bugging,
gradually mummified into smog.
   The coat of arms? –
   A heavy one, hanging
   from the eyelids, from the lips,
   and nostrils of this planet,
   a rusty padlock:
   p a r a g r a p h
    §

(1988)

Under whose sky

I look feelingly into the future.

Nothing is interned in its alloted place.
I mistake myself for my shadow
melted down into crowds,

stretching its arms to the armless shadow
of a former tree –
under whose sky?

The whirlwind of passing each other sweeps up
like rubbish the crumbly leaf-fall
in the underpasses of my muse chronicles.

Through a chink in the tunnel, thinner than a hair,
a – I can't quite see what,
yet it glows faintly.

(1988)

Strength

I'm stronger as I am.
I have nothing that can be taken from me.
Nothing of mine that makes me tremble in fear.
Nothing to lock away in silence.
I don't watch furtively in case of theft.
I can stand fearless facing
the winds of the world.
Come on winds, lash out at me!
What more can you take from me?
I've no burden of my own to carry
so you won't be able to deform me.
I beg to keep nothing personally
so you won't force me to my knees.
I hold nothing in my cupped hands
so you won't be able to shackle me.

I'm free now,
with unfettered wings and thoughts,
so I'm able to embrace everything.
The more you take from me, world,
the more I possess you.
And you'll belong to me
more than ever before, world,
when I stop possessing myself.

To the end

If everything is explained, proved, and calculated,
if the whole planet turns
into a fireball of a super brain
all-seeing, all-hearing, all-knowing,
one thing will remain unexplained to the end:
that human longing for something different,
> a different time,
> a different way,
> a different place.

(1988)

From one myth to another

Man was carved out of a stone,
hurled from an alien star.

If he were put together from clay –
as the biblical myth goes –
at the first blow
he'd disintegrate into tears and mud,
particles in a mud pack
and the tinkle of broken speech;
into ashes of cupped hands
and smoke from the heart.

He wouldn't even reach
the great-great grandstone age.

If he were carved from earth's granite –
like the colossus of some cult –
he'd crumble in the course of time,
due to sharp-toothed erosion,
and then cover the ocean bed
with illusions crushed into sand,
passions ground to silt
into depths without a trace.

But harder than any stone
is the mollusc called man.

Harder even than a fossil.
He bears the harshest shocks in life, breaking up
the home, love, faith,
name, roads, eyes, life.
But he's got one weakness:
He can't bear to hear a word said against him
and so throws himself from the skyscraper –
mythically heavy and hard.

As if hurled like a stone
against this sinful Earth with a curse.

(1987)

Flocks heading south

A part of me,
    always looking for warmth
    but there was never enough here.

A part of me,
    harmonious with the dawned light of day
    yet always locked in shadows of dream.

A part of me,
    which could fly
    but never found its own sky.

A part of me –
    the *me*-est with the eyes of a child
    flies away, flies with flocks to the south.

(1984)

Touch

Two people touching each another,
    doomed to love one another,
    is wounding.

Repelling each other
    is scratching the wound
    till it bleeds.

Whatever they do
    to each other out of love –
    hurts.

This binds them together blindfolded.
    And the only remedy
    is the pain.

I know only too well.

(March 88)

But

Meeting after life-long parting.
Winter under gnawed stars.
You feel like fleeing –
    But

time flows towards the spring.
The first wet snow on your hair
bears the smell of first things.
One look pours matured thirst into another.
    But

a crumble of ice tinkles in the glass
and sticks in the throat scorching.
Senior age and infant youth –
how similar they are
with this choking, unconquerable
    But.

There's meeting after parting, there's
an instant where the BUT is refuted.
If only you can live to see it!
    But . . .

(1988)

35

Limpidness

Now I've got a foretaste of those limits of love,
where it never vows change,
never swallows fire, never promises the moon
never rattles a life-time chain,
never tipsies with the wormwood wine of relish,
never threatens with that most generous gift – a child,
never howls in pain, never flares at a word,
never causes a world catastrophe,
never suicides hope with a look, –
those limpid, so limpid limits,
where love is just a feeling,
deep as the last breath.

(1987)

Notepad under the pillow

I drag it out at dawn
from the depths of dreams.

My hand has scribbled,
uninhibited in darkness.

I can hardly read the signs
of that runic script.

I've sent myself messages
from somewhere out there.

And morning grows clearer
from their unclearness.

(1988)

The Madonna from Russe

To a mother of self-sacrifice

Under medical care in a sterile hell,
screaming in labour

a woman aborts the future.

But it fights back – a clot of blood,
clings deep to the womb,
hoping for mercy from its mother
and praying in desperate morse:

– let me see the sun!

But she doesn't want it to grow
without air, without song, without swallows,
without the spread of a window's wings,
without a crunchy apple to bite into,
without the wonders of snow and blossom,
without being able to run barefoot by the river,
without an open free face,
without laughter, without memory, without faith.

And the unfulfilled future fades away

And the sun – a clot of blood –
is wrapped in black swaddling clothes.
And in the yellow chloride fog
this ghost-town haunts.

Child murderous maternity.

Forgive me these powerless words!
The Danube flows into a tear.

(8 March, 1988)

(The Romanian Chloride Plant of Giurgiu, situated on the border opposite
the Bulgarian town of Russe on the Danube, has been poisoning the area
with its pollution, causing some congenital deformities.)

Experience

There is no trace
of those monumental celebrations.

Everything is transient,
but the most transient
is what we call eternal:
friendship,
fame,
power,
success,
victory.

Only the most fragile lasts:
a deep scar left by you, Love.

Amnesty

Through the eyelashes of sleep
to meet the dawn in your lover's eyes.
The morning shines having drunk stars.

It is complete amnesty
from fierce nightmares
of tyrannosaurus-darkness.

And our condemned world
explodes into laughter at a word
and is set free.

And loners whom love
by-passes indifferently –
Is the world doomed to have them?

Love, have you no mercy?

(1987)

In memory . . .

Before he was born, before that first breath,
before he cried out, he died.

My older brother, before he grew strong,
before his shoulder towered to protect me.

Before he could shield me from those behind my back
casting the evil eye, words and stones.

Before he could take me to my first dance
with his best friend as my partner.

Before leaning over my head to see my maths,
being more mature – to help me get it right.

Before he accompanied me caringly in the teeming train
of my difficult trip through life.

To wait for me at least once in the darkness at some station
to take my luggage, to say – welcome back!

And to feel a brotherly hand over the chasm.
And the miracle, each moment – to breathe.

I drink down my brother's space.

(1988)

Family legend

Now it's all the rage
to trace your family tree
(because of an inferiority complex).

And I search for my roots
like a felled tree.
But they stop at grandfather
at that great family story,
often recalled amid laughter:

At his betrothal with my grandmother
(a beauty for those days),
for the blessing
the bridegroom carried
his paralysed mother on his back
up the steep little streets of Tarnovo
to the bride's house on the heights of Varusha,
sweat streaming from him.

I don't need anything else.
That means more to me
than a whole gallery
of important ancestors.
And Grandfather died young.
As a child I would imagine
him climbing up to Heaven
with his mother on his back,
the streams running from his forehead
turning to warm rain.

And this retro trickle
almost as a joke, waters
my dried up days.

(1988)

Hopefully

Hopefully the moment won't catch you,
having ended everything,
having crowned your dreamed-up opus
with a full-stop –
like a nail driven into masonry. –

Hopefully that moment like a guest
at a jubilee will not fell you –
you who have wreathed those sweet dreams,
right up to the end,
like a bravura chord.

And not a word unspoken to the end,
and not a line uncrossed out to the end,
and not an idea abandoned
for the next
step towards the unthought of completeness.

This means
that long before you had conceived yourself,
you were already finished
with not a single seed to germinate
in the expectant earth.

Hopefully the moment won't outrun you.

(1986)

Snow

Snow falls, snow upon snow.
My mother leads a small child by the hand.
Those tiny footprints in the snow are mine.

Snow falls from my childhood, snow upon snow.
I lead a small girl by the hand.
These footprints in the snow are yours, daughter.

A white blanket spreads across a fresh grave.
Whose are those footprints in the deep snow?
Snow falls covering the steps, snow upon snow.

(1988)

To you

You still expect me
to utter the one thing
I cannot utter.

This expectation
that wakes the pain-word
in the severed tongue.

Thus with a change of weather
an amputated leg hurts
impatient to set off on the way.

(1988)

Most

I lived in the most golden of ages,
I lived in the fairest system
under the wisest doctrine,
with the highest morality,
amid the most eternal friendship,
in the happiest society,
towards the most wonderful future.

I skipped the comparative *more*,
and found myself straight into *most*.
It was compulsory for a smile
to be most blissfully radiant,
a moment – the most historic,
a feast – the most festive,
progress – the most progressive.

I believed with the most genuine belief,
I glowed with the most glowing glow,
and I always rose on tip-toe
to over-stretch at the high jump: most, most.
It's just that I don't know why
my poems became so sad
and sadder and sadder towards the end.

(1 October, 1990)

Fate

But a moment comes when
Fate will knock on the door
with your own hand.

You've no choice but to answer.
And silence is driven off
by your own voice.

Whatever was written in the stars –
you'll write again yourself
with your own unsteady script.

And if you strike it out in fear,
you will delete your own face
with your own stroke.

Fate passes into you.
And where can you run to
further than your own skin?

(1 January, 1989)

I saw

I saw my assassin.
I saw him close to.
Made to measure
for punches below the belt.
I saw his fingers.
I saw them close to.
Dangerously infantile
gripping the glass
and me by the throat.
I saw his teeth.
I saw them close to.
Like a demolished wall.
I spoke to this wall,
But I never saw his eyes.
Even from afar.
Behind dark glasses –
a blind man at the crossroads.
I had a strange feeling
of pain and fear
almost as if he'd been
a brother.
I saw my assassin.

(6 February, 1989)

Talking in your sleep

Harmony is impaired.
Don't try to play an ode
on the harp of my nerves!
Right at the climax
a nerve tears
and a rending dissonance sounds.
When, how, why
did we demolish harmony?
One hurtful false-note after another.
The vast harmonium of humanity
is at pains to perform
The Ode to Joy.
But one after another
chords tear with a scream,
one after another
threads unravel with a groan.
Stuff your ears
with smoker's cottonwool!
Joy sounds ominous.
Harmony is impaired.
Surgeons, suture the nerves
with green threads of grass!
Tuners, replace the chords
with sunbeams!
Weavers, interweave the threads
with tired maternal fingers!
Without falseness, without violence,
without heart-plucking children's cries,
the crushed harmonium of humanity
cannot possibly perform
The Ode to Joy.

(1977)

If

When you return,
    if you return –
and not until, you'll see your own absence.

All roads will run
    in countless directions,
and only yours will be stopped.

Your words of greeting –
    confused, downcast –
will be as from a stranger.

You will step inside guiltily,
    to look around
as if in a forgotten home, seen in a dream.

And your fingers will touch
    your own absence
in the misplaced books and objects.

And you will realise that
    things are misplaced
not only in your own home but in the world.

Simply and quite naturally –
    so they'll fill
the space you used to occupy.

(December 1973)

Under the snow

– I have this sense of incompleteness –
he said at the last rendezvous,
staring out at the falling snow.

I was about to respond, but remained silent.

Both of us were in a hurry to miss . . .
Summer lured us with eternity,
pouring down sandy moons.
They seeped through our fingers.

Maybe it's better this way.

The pain of incompleteness,
this part-drunk love of ours
to go babbling on under white snow,

dreaming its unfinished dream.

(1 October, 1990)

An old song to a new tune

Each new love is an assassin –
without turning a hair
it wipes out all previous ones
with oh such an innocent smile
it knifes the only love,
the last and the first!

Accomplices are everywhere:
A late bus at the bus-stop,
a sudden shower, and many more.
Freedom is Love's alibi.

This rendezvous is an escape from yourself.
This feast a memorial service
that Death attends incognito.
The moment it ceases to be new
there's another love round the corner
with a knife.

But the late hour strikes.
And you realize that love,
as in days gone by, has been crushed
into new, newer, newest and so on . . .

(1985)

Tomorrow

Tomorrow, mirage-like, longed for.
My life has been a vow
to the legendary spectre of a Tomorrow.

Godless sacrifices,
a Now mercilessly postponed
for an eternally distant Tomorrow.

Ah, how many unquaffed sunsets,
or moons, you've turned your back on –
just for Tomorrow, my undawned Tomorrow!

And who, hidden in faceless shadow,
is again about to steal
your zeal gratis, Tomorrow?

And how will Yesterday's scarecrows
steal by mimicry
into the blurring, dawning twilight?

You can never become Today.
You turn into foul Yesterday.
And I believe only in you – Tomorrow!

(30 October, 1989)

Fragmentation

Fragmented personality divided
into together   and yet not whole,
into yesterday   and never,
into home   and nowhere,
into name   and no one,
into face   and nonentity,
into voice   and no voice,
into perhaps   and no way –
Could it ever be made whole?

Repentance

He stood before me howling, the executioner.
And his cry was excruciating.
He cupped his hands suddenly
as if holding a severed head.

His whole body shuddered silently
weeping in tearless convulsions.

A heavy minute rolled past
and bathed my heart in blood.

Then a prayer
broke out on my lips:

'Oh, God, please don't let my punishment
be that I make the beheader die!

Forgive my involuntary forgiveness
of this accursed cry!'

(10 May, 1989)

Announcement

I am looking for my smile.
I dropped it somewhere around here
between the facts and the phrases.

Whoever finds it,
tell them to use it
as a string-ring on their little finger!

And say to the punisher:
Stop these pretenders causing pain!
He who promotes fear panics.

(8 April, 1989)

I hear a cry

I forget my child,
I reject my text,
I neglect my home –
I hear a desperate cry.

Crossed out text,
you are my small child,
my pillaged home on fire –
My Motherland, crying out for help.

But what on earth can I do
with two helpless hands?
For me the only surge of strength
is your dreadful cry for help.

(1989)

Night diary

Time turned upside down.
Day becomes night, night – day.
An alarm clock wakes me from my vigil.

Pain erupts into stars at mid-day.
I sprinkle the midnight word
– biting salt, onto a burning wound.

The dead breathe life into me.
I guide myself as if blind
across chaotic crossroads.

Out of darkness will come the light.

(9 October 1991)

Sysiphus

To Vaclav Havel

When hope comes true,
it's only then you realize,
that you've never really hoped.

What an unheard of miracle:
Sysiphus, did you really push
the boulder to the very top?

And still the boulder doesn't crash
down in the ravine,
as the ancient myth demands . . .

Why aren't you triumphant?
Have you grown into the habit
of pushing the boulder until breathless?

Do you enjoy
the chafing rough edges
which make your palms sore?

You've a sad smile, why?

Or do you want something more impossible:
like balancing that boulder on the ridge,
that took such toil to get it to the top?

Now you measure its weight
with the scales of anxiety,
with the crucifixion of thought.

Not a boulder! but petrified history,
humiliations, battles and pain,
a petrified fate of a people.

59

Ah, will you ever manage to balance
that shaken and battered granite
overhanging the abyss?

Sysiphus and victory – absurdity!

Today your pains on the cross
are a show for the screen –
the hundred-headed dragon, this world, watches you.

If you were to pull away an arm
in order to jot down the drama
that now rises within you,

the granite would fall,
and hope scatter
into thousands of dramas and sorrows.

If you desert into yourself –
where orphan laughter
calls out to you weeping,

the boulder will drag you
down into the abyss,
crushed by remorse.
Beware – that they don't marble-ize you!

Sysiphus, with a curse
you are doomed to the stone,
so as to inspire soul into it.

(30 September, 1990)

Fingerprints

Murdered, tenderness murdered.

I discover
murderers' fingerprints
everywhere:

in the exhalation of air,
in the sawdust tan of bread,
in the twilight of a glass of water.

I am followed by the fingerprints
of back-sliders,
by the blind page filled with script.

But the accomplices'
worst vileness is stained fast
on the dead silence.

And who can't see themselves there?

(1988)

In defiance

At dawn
let the bell-tower of the lark
wake me young!

So my eyes will unlock
to the many tos and fros
that become rendezvous

with the smile's
prototype, with the theomachy of poplars,
with mutuality itself.

In defiance of you,
explicitness, in defiance of everything irreversible,
of causal connections

in defiance of sober minds!

(15 April, 1989)

Eulogy of the missed hare

The missed hare
is still whole and is hiding
in the unknown thicket.
He himself bulges out
all those scraggy thorns
with breathing probability.
Let him live!

(1988)

Fallen from the moon

Heavier and heavier, I climb the stairs.
I pause for breath to catch me up.
I have a strange problem with gravitation.
It's as if I've fallen from the moon
once I leapt to with ease.

(1988)

Between

I remember an old belief from my native village:

Never turn a soul back once it's set off for the beyond,
or it'll never settle.

I was returned forcefully – no one's shadow,
hanging under noon's sky on a beam
      between

the earth – a warm and dusky hollow,
swarming with bees, stings and honey –

and a bright chasm of silence.
Rocked slightly on its torn breath
      between

the illusory tangibility of things
and the word's forcefield –

In the ringing space of solitude,
where each colourful desire
      between

this side and the beyond cuts it into snow.

(1988)

Books

Books – looked for, grabbed, stacked,
      even more fiercely grab
      the air in my paper molehill.

And if an able hand
      ever turns back the course of time
      backwards, far backwards . . .

Let books whirl in annual rings,
      and paper stream as pulp magma,
      and minced pages sprout leaves.

Let heavy volumes be knotted into roots,
      bindings stretch out as trunks,
      and century-old shadows shoot up high.

Let the dusty shelves crown into branches,
      let revived forests start to rustle
      from libraries' non-existence.

And let me, a child, unguarded, lost in the forest
      plunge into whispering mystery,
      still unaware of fear.

And long before the anthill of letters swarm,
      let me learn the language of the birds,
      and let the cuckoo countdown my life:

One, two or three more last green years.
      until I plunge into the crevices of books,
      looking between the lines of yellowing pages

for the disobedient sprite.

(1988)

Clouds

A cloudless sky – desert in blue.
A glassy false eye.

It has no intention of bursting
into even a single tear, to thunder into rage.

Beads of the promised bride to be
glisten dully, joylessly.

You're drowned, sky, in your own celestial blue.

From the clouds you take on shape,
and the depth and essence of sky.

Inconstant in the fluent cadence
they untie my imagination.

My eyes set off after their caravan
and I am a bedouin, a plaiter of parables.

An oracle about winged contraptions,
a discoverer of transformations.

You weigh heavy, sky, having shouldered a storm.

And a certain euphoria boils over
into the steep river valley of blood.

Sheet lightning! It'll thunder! It'll lash down!
I stretch my palm upwards.

How did this ancient gesture flow into me?

I receive the first forecasting spot.

On my palm – the infinity of being.

(1988)

One day

If one day, one of my countless days
could be repeated –
which would I choose?

All those I remember clearly,
the so-called 'unforgettable',
seem alien to me.
I am outside them,
for I watch them from the side,
images reassessed –
in the undrained well of memory.

The unremembered – these are my real days.
I belong to them
and am still within them.
They hold the whole of me
in the web of their air
imperceptible, luminous, saturated
with the honey-bearing sensation
of a life lived in a dream.

I would trade all my dear memories
for one forgotten day.

Just an ordinary day, drowned
in scattered day-light.
To taste again
its simple insignificance,
its serene fullness,
unruffled by anything memorable.

To be drunk again
with the undoctored juice
of a dreamed-up world
and then to forget it forever.

(Stockholm, 1969)

68

Almost prophecy

To Konstantin Pavlov

And the hour of the word shall strike
when you least expect it.

And truth shall thunder
like spring rain on a tin roof.

And the rivers of words shall start to flow
upwards, upwards back to the spring.

And the stones shall stir
and each settle into its proper place.

And the trees shall weep
and reach up towards the stars with severed fingers.

And the flowers shall rise again
and each shall sigh with its own breath.

And the birds shall return
and with their beaks shall melt the ice into song.

And the graves shall break open
        and pierced skulls
shall ring like Easter bells.

And retribution shall be sought
for each evil deed or lie.

Yet there shall be no blood-shedding,
        only blood-transfusing
through the healing blade of the word.

(1977)

Claustrophobia

For our minds –
        as high as possible
        and pre-cast sky-scrapable
        walls

For the word –
        as secretive as possible
        and seven times lockable
        locks.

For the gestures –
        as skyless as possible
        and wasp-hiveable
        cells.

For the look –
        as century-old as possible
        and lopped off
        trees.

For the imagination –
        if it's still to be seen –
        the screen
        of a blind wall.

Space –
        ultradangerous infinity.
        Before you know it,
        we're up there
        shining
with our own light.

(1977)

God's bird

– Come down from the clouds for lunch –
my father calls.

I throw to the floor the white down
of my poems.

I sit at the table. My hair –
a dishevelled kite.

I look up – under the eyelashes
stolen azure.

And on the lips – my mother's
tastiest soup

And her snow-white laundry flutters
from the balcony.

And everything that flies will land
in my cupped hands.

No problem – to ride the clouds
and fly away

straight to that radiant chasm
known as future.

(1988)

Impatience

Man is impatience.
He's born pushing towards the day
through his mother's wound.
And all his life
blood circulation jostles him
to hurry up, not to be late,
to reach the final limit
as soon as possible.
And panting, exhausted
with the last impatience,
himself turned into a wound,
he passes through himself
towards the dead of night beyond.

Why is he so impatient?
Who even more impatient calls him?

(1976)

With a look from afar

The sea is flooded
by the deeper sea of darkness.
The only proof
of any presence of a sea
is the rhythmic lapping
and the foamy, unfathomable wind.

Damp, drowning sorrow pierces.
From a distance how it lures
that moving light.
Perhaps some loner
unreeled the rope from the wharf,
disentangled the most evil of knots
and sailed off brave and free.

I would give up everything just to be there now!

And from a distance
does he peer at my lit window
with the longing of the homeless,
and does he ever ask who's at home
crouching under the lamp
reading in the warmth, so calmly?

Would he give up everything to be here now?

(1988)

Secondary blooming

In the late autumn – a chestnut in bloom.
A yellow leaf-fall and cranes leaving.
And on branches – the wig of spring.

The white candles of the Slavonic Church blaze.
Is it for a wedding or a funeral?
Or an old bachelor's dreams come true?

Or wisdom parodied in reckless blossom?
The chestnut dares to infringe
the despotic irreversible circle.

The executioner stalks him with a hood of fog.
Leaves like weather-men whisper forecasts
of unrecorded wolf-frost winter.

All white, doomed to self-blackening,
it is an appealing omen in the town
for a lurking burst of opposition.

Risk is always an anomaly.

In the resigned autumn – a chestnut in bloom.
An unheard of miracle, alarm and hope.
One summer when pigs flew it burst its buds out of spite.

(1988)

Unconscious

Darkness thickened around us
        (literally and figuratively speaking),
And light grew up in your eyes.
An arm's length was a distance
we never dared melt.

So we unconsciously drank
silence like life-saving air
        (the tongue rashed from words).
And both of us were illuminated
with a harmonious extra-wordy speech.

For an instant I felt that celestial closeness
        (when earth's not enough – celestial),
which moves all luminaries,
keeping them at a distance –
to be eternally attracted and to burn.

        (the eternal is also relative)

(1988)

A handful of dust on you all, who
used to love me.
As I sprinkle ashes on live embers
in a hearth.

Let your eyes smoulder in the dark night
'til next time we meet.
Nowhere else do I exist
more beautiful and more expected.

A handful of dust for words
which I never uttered.
A handful of dust from the earth to the earth –
everyone's nuptial bed.

More and more cold, more and more a desert
without you around.
More and more distant, you
who truly loved me.

A handful of dust on your cupped hands –
warm and full of forgiveness,
before they fly away – birds of passage
thrill when alighting on my shoulder.

(1991)

A spiral staircase – Life.
I naively believed I was climbing
without stepping on anyone's shoulder.

Actually each step is a shoulder.
Shadow built upon shadow.
Steep cascades of swollen feet.

Throngs of Cariatids.

They climb heavily upwards.
Stairs of generations
they carry the followers on their shoulders.

A Babylonian tower of human shoulders.

Increasingly bent double. Increasingly breathless.
And on the verge of reaching the upper floor,
the carrier collapses to become another step.

The step is still warm. But look, the next
has already stepped on the wretched shoulders.
Perhaps he will reach the dome.

And beyond the dome,
through the opening beyond,
the spiral staircase of the Milky Way will half open . . .

Staircase – an old hunchbacked centipede.
Once I flew from shoulder to shoulder
then bent my own back as a beast of burden

for others to climb.

(1991)

With the latchkey of the Word
I wanted to open the blocked road.

With the key of ancient myths
I wanted to open today.

With the key of Bach's oratorios
I wanted to open chaos.

With the key of hypnotic slogans
I wanted to open the heart.

It doesn't fit! It sticks!

With the key of theory
I wanted to open social progress.

With the key of self-proclaimed reason
I wanted to open Nature.

With the key of success
I wanted to open happiness.

With the skeleton key of promises
I wanted to open the future.

It jams! It refuses to turn!

Tell me, prophets, minstrels, philosophers,
which of these is the right key?

(1991)

Winter seeds

Let the Word survive so Bulgaria
will last forever!

Sofia, 1 January, 1992

Speaking of unspoken words.

*

The field sleeps, having pulled a fleecy rug of snow
over its head,
dreaming of waif seeds.
We sowed the whole land with words.
What will sprout in Spring?

*

Woods heavy with snow
are deep in thought
on what one keeps silent about to the end.

*

Exile –
to be a poor translator of yourself.
You don't exist in a foreign language.
You'd find it easier
to be deaf and dumb.

*

Small and spiteful snowflakes
push me back sharply.
And landing on my shoulder
become a white wing –
With it I glide forwards.

*

Who has Beethoven's deafness
to hear the divine notes?

*

More dreadful
than blindness
is to see
how tormented this land is.

*

Someone's absence,
more and more tangibly,
fills the space around you.
An absence
without which everything is pointless.

*

History writes with your footprints
in the fresh snow
that which was written for you.
Nothing happens of its own accord.
So, don't stop, walk on
against this snow wall.

*

When my shadow lengthens in the evening,
the world about me grows silent.
Stretches from the end of my path
as if someone expects me there . . .
The shadows take me far away
without a hint of where.

*

My land is where
my words weigh heavy.

(1992)